impressions

selected verses

jesse s. smith

℘

basementia publications

impressions: selected verses
Jesse S. Smith

First printing September 2022

Published by Basementia Publications
Silverton, Oregon
www.basementia.com • jessesmithbooks.com

Hardcover ISBN 978-1-958337-02-8

Cover image based on hand stencil cave painting at Pech Merle Cave in Le Lot, France. Photo sourced from Wikipedia (Public Domain).

File under Poetry / Song Lyrics

For my wonderful wife, Jessica.
It just keeps getting better

Foreword

These collected verses were composed over the course of more than three decades, from my youth into middle age.

Individually, the verses are impressions of images and feelings. Viewed together, they may suggest the blurred outline of a life story, the way splatters of pigment blown around a hand may leave a hand-shaped impression on the wall of a prehistoric cave.

Many of these songs have been performed live and on recordings through the years; and I am grateful to all who have listened, jammed with me, and sang along.

Wishing you great joy.

~Jesse S. Smith
October 25, 2020

Part 1: Juvenilia

(1987 to 1995) – *Twelve to Twenty*

ଓଛ

The Knight and the Dragon

Late at night, I hear this knight
    Goin' off to kill a dragon.
His armor is oiled, his sword is new,
    And along his girlfriend is taggin'

Now lemme tell you 'bout this dragon:
He breathes fire in front, his tail is draggin' –
    His skin, it's green,
    And man, this guy is mean!
He takes all the girls and he sticks them in a cave,
And there they have to sit, 'til they die of old age.

The knight sets up his lance,
Tells the dragon he hasn't a chance,
    And tells his horse to charge –
I won't tell you 'bout the fight,
Let's say it's not a pretty sight:
    The dragon is surprisingly large!

Pandora's Box

It was opened long ago,
      long before I was alive,
and it set loose all the plagues
      which still beset mankind.

Demons leapt from the box
      like ugly, vicious rats:
greed, fear, selfishness,
      hatred, like a thousand bats.

Taking root in humans, these pests
      could now flourish and grow,
And before they kill us all,
      we must exterminate them now!

Help us close Pandora's Box!
Help us close Pandora's Box!
We need a key that fits the lock,
so help us close Pandora's Box!

Stupid Jerks

Saw my old love with a slimy guy
I'm not really jealous, I just wish he'd die
Why would she date a football-playing jock
Who drives a big truck and thinks with his cock?

You beautiful women who date stupid jerks
I try to understand but it makes my brain hurt
Why won't you leave him when he treats you like dirt?
You're a beautiful woman, but he's a stupid jerk!

Normal

I wear shades to cover my eyes
so I can continue to lie
"oh, I'm fine no problems I'm normal"

sometimes I think nobody is normal
we're all just amateur actors
pretend we're fine
act problem- free
exhibit normality
for an inattentive audience

Flowers in Her Hair

Riding the wave
   up to the clouds
There's no today,
   there's only now

The mountains smile,
   the trees they bough
The river runs
   to show me how

The meaning of life
   taught to me there
in a green field
   by the girl with flowers in her hair

And the insects sing
   with a certain delight
They don't care if it's
   day or night

'Cause the planet spins
   'neath the open sky
If you listen close
   they'll tell you why

Coffee

Time
  flits by
  floats before me

I sip
  again
  my brew
  hot water dripped through ground seeds

Morning
  ticks away
While I sit
 and sip.

Power

Imagine
the way Jimi Hendrix must have felt
towards the untimely end of his career
about songs like *Purple Haze*
that everybody wanted to hear:
playing a song like that
to a packed stadium,
with the effects turned all the way
up to eleven;
a real showstopper piece
that everyone knows so well
you can improvise off its theme,
implying the notes,
taking a solo spot
which climaxes
in a personal specialty
- explosions of sound -
then closing the number
with a massive,
thunderous
musical strut
before the curtains
and a final bow.

Kind Weed: An Ode

O! For buds so green,
My baggie with them full;
Glass bong hits are so keen!
'Tis with these my mind I annul.

Aligned, am I! My folks be sad;
What's wrong with me, and why?
Nay, nay, stay; I turn not to bad
The drive is in me to be HIGH!

For men there be (it seems to me)
Who rarely feel high enough;
It's a lifestyle, you see; for Jonesers are we
Who feel that life need not be rough!

Looking Back

I have cut myself
  with a knife
And bludgeoned my brain
  with bottles

My ears have suffered
  decibel damage
And my throat has been
    shredded
   by hours of screaming

I have pounded my head on walls
  And bruised my fist
   on a locker
    in high school

I have shorted my circuits
   to bounce colors
     to feel worthy
    and to dance with the stars

I have blackened my lungs
   trying to prove I have power
    over fire
    and my life
    but only succeeded in proving
      powerless

Have I reached the end yet?
In taking out frustrations on myself
  have I finished
  squelching the voice in the background?

There is always more.
The voice will never be silent.
I hear it now
   saying
   no matter how happy I am
   I will never be
   satisfied.

Part 2: Four-Track Life

(1995 to 1997) – *Twenty to Twenty-Two*

ॐ ♫ ॐ

Armor Amour

I want to be your knight in shining armor
    Riding across the moor
I want to be your prince with a glass slipper, singin'
    "Slave for your stepmother no more"

I want to be your Perseus
    Save you from monsters of the deep
I'll swoop down on my wingèd steed
    And duel with some evil creep

And when you go to sleep at night
    I'll be the moon that shines on your face
And when you go to sleep at night
    I dream of being your dream

Ooh, I want to be your fairy tale
Ooh, I dream of being your dream

I want to be your knight in shining armor
    I hope that wherever you are
You know I can always reach you
    With my magic guitar

Affirmation

I am less common than one in a million
I'm my own person, and I will stand tall
I can fight like a lion
or cry like a man
but I'll never surrender
or quit saying who I am!

Gonna Be OK

Smiles come your way
It's a beautiful day
You hear what I say
You're gonna be okay

Minimum Wage

While I'm washin' dishes
I keep makin' wishes
Yeah I'm earnin' some money
but I'm thinkin' of you, honey
I'm just washin' these dishes
and I'm makin' wishes
        and I'm waitin' for the shift to end

Minimum wage,
minimum wage,
minimum wage,
I'm makin' minimum wage

The boss she says, "Quit dreamin'!"
The water is a-steamin'
I feel, oh, so tired
but I can't afford to get fired.
The boss she says, "Quit dreamin'!"
The water is a-steamin'
        and I'm waitin' for the shift to end.

Minimum wage,
Minimum wage,
Minimum wage,
I'm makin' minimum wage

The Oregon Country Fair

She said, "I'll take you to a place
    that will blow your mind"
So we left those city lights
    far behind

Now it's been too long
    since I've been back there
So meet me by the bridge
    at the Oregon Country Fair!

There's endless possibilities
    you may find
So let us participate
    in the great unwind

No I just can't wait
    to go back there
So meet me by the bridge
    at the Oregon Country Fair!

I'm waiting for the girl
    with flowers in her hair
She said to meet her by the bridge
    at the Oregon Country Fair

The Greeting

Say "hello" to the sun
　　and the birds in the trees
Say "hello" to the clouds
　　and the flowers and me

　　Hello! Hello!
　　Ba doodn da doot dah
　　Ba dweedle a doot dee
　　It's a lovely day!

Thank You All

I want to say thank you
    thank you to everyone who has been kind to me
    thank you to everyone who has loved me
    thank you to everyone who has smiled at me
    thank you to everyone
        who has treated me
           the way all human beings
              should treat each other.
              Let's all
            treat each other
            treat each other
        the way we all should.

Let's hear everybody say, "Peace!"
Yeah!

Regret

I met you at a party
and it was getting late
you could have been the perfect girl for me
but I did hesitate

I wish I'd asked for your phone number

No, I wasn't thinking right
Yes, I did something wrong
'Cause you left for the night
and now I'm singin' this song

I should have asked for your phone number

I don't remember what we talked about
I don't remember your name
Now you're not here when the lights go out
and I think it's such a shame

I should have asked for your phone number!

The Wank Song

Masturbating is good clean fun
Masturbating is good clean fun
Beating off is fun for one
Having a wank is fun for one

"You know, it's really amazing how much value modern science can pack into a single word. It's not a very pretty word, but it sure says a lot. This one word can turn your life around. And so I say:"

Masturbating is easy to do
It's fun for one when there are not two
Masturbating doesn't spread disease
like AIDS and babies and genital fleas

Masturbating is legally fun
you can pretend to sleep with anyone
It's so easy when you know how
I think I'll go do it right now

Aliens

When the aliens came
we were taken by surprise
for we had never seen
anything quite their size

Well, we thought that our life
on Earth was getting droll
until the aliens
started eating us whole

And now we're going down
to the bottom of the food chain

Your Reality

Hey, wonderful woman
    I'm so glad to see you've come
Do you have time to tell me
    'bout the world that you are from?

What is it like,
    the life you call your own?
What do you do
    in the place that you call home?

Is it very far away?
Tell me, do you plan to stay?
So glad you're with me today,
life is better when we play!

Do things I never notice
    fill your attention through the day?
Do the things that concern me most
    in your eyes sort of fade away?

Tell me of your reality
Tell me of the life you lead
Tell me of the world you see
Tell me who you want to be

Part 3: Mourning and Maturing

(1997-2000) – *Twenty-Two to Twenty-Five*

A Koan

Each winter,
     more rocks come up in the fields;
Each spring,
     more flowers.

Carryin' It

Balance exists in nature
Balance exists within
Balance exists in nature
Balance exists within

Scales may be tipped
they criticize,
they tellin' lies,
and you slipped
But when everything goes wrong
just remember the song
and keep carryin' on

If You...

If you were a bird
    you could teach me to fly
and if you were a star
    you'd be up in the sky

If you were a statue
    you'd be made out of gold
and if you were the Devil
    I'd sell you my soul

Baby you're the best
    at everything you do
Oh girl, can't you see
    that's why I've fallen for you

Duncan's Quest

Young Duncan the page boy
    trudged down the lane
He ran the same errand every day
    and now he was doing it again

He wanted to run to the hills
    and enjoy the nice day
Instead he had to work
    for a pitiful pay

He wished again that he could be free
    and thought, "Life just ain't fair!"
As he was thinkin' about climbing a tree
    he walked into the town square

And there was a band of wandering minstrels
    set up on the corner to play
with a hat set by for generosity
    This is what their song did say:

"Follow the rainbow
 Follow the rainbow
 Don't let your dreams go
 You gotta follow the, follow the – "

Duncan on a quest, yeah
Duncan on a quest
    for the rainbow

Sing It

Well, there are so many things
    going wrong with the world
        I don't know what we're gonna do
It seems like there is no hope,
    too many problems to cope
        but if you asked me for suggestions, I'd have a few

Hey, everybody, take some time
to enjoy your life while you've got it
Let yourself be amazed by the world around you
and sing a happy tune

Because we all need to sing
    la la la la la la
And we all need to smile
    hey hey hey hey hey
and we all need some love
    do do be do be do
Think about it a while

One day I talked with a guy
    who said he wanted to die,
        he thought his life was at a dead end.
I told him, "Don't get too down,
    the sun will come back around
        don't forget to be your own best friend"

Everybody needs some space
to live a life that makes them happy
So let yourself be amazed by the world around you
and sing a happy tune

Because we all need to sing
    la la la la la la
And we all need to smile
    hey everybody smile
and we all need some love
    love everybody, love yourself
Think about it a while

The Pensive Pooch

What does my dog think about?
What does my dog think about?
Does he who what when, where why how?
What does my dog think about?

What does his life mean to him?
Does he act on his every whim?
Does he wonder what happens when you die?
Does he invent principles to justify?

What does my dog think about?
What does my dog think about?
Does he who what when, where why how?
What does my dog think about?

Does he reminisce a lot
to the days before he was bought?
Or the time he got in a spat
with that mean ol' tomcat?

What does my dog think about?

Canvas

The artist paints her canvas
 the colors swirl round
They move zigzag from side to side
 but never make a sound

The artist paints her canvas
 the warmth of afterglow
The gold of joy, a rosy-cheeked boy,
 and places she will go

The artist paints her canvas
 all the rosy hues of love
The faded jade, the midnight shade
 the blue sky up above

The artist paints her canvas
 the images are vague
On the brink of indistinct
 and quietly they fade

For on the artists' canvas
 possibilities combine
The love of life, the zib zab zife!
 These things all intertwine

I Sleep Better

(In the Style of a 70's Slow-Funk Song,
with heavy strings, and a deep bass groove up front in the mix)

When we make love, you know it's so full of meaning
Sometimes we want something more
I need a new way to tell you I love you
Because I've said those words before

Words have certain limitations
There are things a touch cannot show
I may say the same things over and over
But I still want you to know

That I sleep better when I'm next to you
I'm so happy with the things you do
I got to tell you 'cause you know it's true
I sleep better when I'm next to you

Words are not enough so
I'll sing them under her window
Until the neighbors start to throw
things at me, I got to go

Moments

A moment lasts forever
 A moment is an eternity long
A moment passes, but there's always another
 moment after it's gone

Each moment an eternity
 come share a moment with me
A lifetime in an instant and gone
 come share a moment with me

A moment lasts a lifetime
 some we cherish and some regret
Each moment a new reality
 some we remember but most we forget

Each moment an eternity
 come share a moment with me
A lifetime is an instant, then gone
 come share a moment with me

Spunky Haste

Drifting slowly from the shore
The current tuggin' it more and more
My box slipped from its resting place
Taking with it my spunky haste

I had been thinkin' all was great!
I didn't notice 'til it was too late –
I ran across the rocky beach;
Stretched from a log, but it was out of reach

I stood in panic and watched it go!
My precious haste, caught in the flow
The water was too cold for a swim
But I summoned my courage and dove on in

Striking outwards from the shore
The current tuggin' me more and more
My jaw clenched 'gainst the bitter chill
My spunky haste eludes me still!

Dream Confessions

In my sleep, in my dream
I was wrapped up in a scene
In the night, in my head
I was lyin' on a bed

If I dreamed of making love
and she didn't look like you
would it mean that I'm unfaithful?
Would you tell me I'm untrue?

Because I wouldn't want to hurt you
You know I want to treat you right
Oh, no, I wouldn't want to tell a lie
in the middle of the night

In my sleep, in my dream
I was wrapped up in a scene
In the night, in my head
I was lyin' on a bed
Oh, baby, I was lyin' on a bed
I was lyin' on a bed
I love your sweet head
Don't want nobody else instead

Faceless Man

Last night I was all alone
with the ringer turned off, on my phone
  I was thinking about something else
    the salty fear
    of a human tear
  and how to save the whales

I was bobbin' my head
my fingers were tappin' the bed
  my eyes closed to concentrate
    If love is wealth,
    is Hell within myself?
  I was hopin' it was not too late

All the concepts left to grasp
of a darkly fateful past
left me pondering in shame
yet still I'm shifting all the blame

My mind wandering afar
my fingers rubbed my chin too hard
it couldn't take so much abuse
a flap of skin it came up loose

So I pulled that flap of skin
and felt it peel off of my chin –
my face responded to the task,
it came off like a rubber mask.

My face just slipped right off my head!
Now I am left faceless instead.
Now I have no identity;
there is no face I wear on me.

Now no one will ever recognize me,
    for I am a faceless man.
I can be whoever you want me to be,
    for I am a faceless man.

I'll blend in with the crowd in the street,
    for I am a faceless man.
You won't notice me in my seat,
    I am a faceless man.

Now nobody will care what I do,
    for I am a faceless man.
I'm walkin' around with one tied shoe,
    I am a faceless man.

Sometimes Closer

Everybody wants a little more
and everyone has felt a slamming door
Together in our solitude
Intertwined futures interlude

Sometimes closer, or farther away
Ooh, la la la, oh, la la la
Longing for bliss every day
Ooh, la la la, oh, la la la

From far to near
From there to here
From yesterday
To next year

Sometimes closer, or farther away
Ooh, la la la, oh, la la la
Longing for bliss every day
Ooh, la la la, oh, la la la

You spend your days pondering
Too aware of everything
Ancient newness and juvenile depth
Transcend limitations with every breath

Sometimes closer, or farther away
Ooh, la la la, oh, la la la
Longing for bliss every day
Ooh, la la la, oh, la la la

Paradise Regained

Paradise in a grain of sand
Paradise in a foreign land
Paradise in a moment and
Paradise lost and gone again

An old man once taught me a spell
It keeps me from going to Hell
Once you find peace within
There is no sin
Just paradise

It's all in the way you see
I'm so glad that your soul can be
Livin' in here with me
Happy in Purgatory

And now I will teach you the spell
It'll keep you from going to Hell
Once you find peace within
There is no sin
Just Paradise

Start the Day (Do It Now)

I gotta rub this sleep right out of my eyes
I gotta get myself more exercise
I gotta find a way to organize my time
so that the life I live will feel like it's mine

Some people say that there is a better way
Some people are just waiting for a better day
In this world of contradictions, you create your own fate
but it will be much worse if we just sit and wait

I wanna help my people see that we're livin' way too fast
and it will help if we can shed ideas from the past
we gotta cut out all our stress and learn to meditate
we got to try to control the chaos we create

Some people are obsessed with their ideas of sin
Some people are just looking for an easy way to win
Some people don't believe that we can turn our world around
Some people won't be satisfied 'til we tear the cities down

I just want a chance to start over again
Oh, yeah, I just want a chance to start over again
Start, start over again, oh, start, whoah –
I just want a chance to start over again

Gold Leaves of the Fall

Now the golden days of Summer
    have turned to gold leaves of the Fall
The sun's rays shine on happy days
    but a cold wind blows through it all

Those people walking all around
Try to deny their common ground
I don't believe in cold reality
I don't live for triviality

Now we go through all our rituals
    and comfort ourselves from fear
The ice and snow are all we know
    but the Spring will soon be here

I love a dirty look on a nice clean face
I love freedom and wide open space
I don't believe in cold reality
I won't live for triviality, oh no

Where Does the Audience Sit?

If all my life is a play
And all I say is a script
And all the world is a stage
Tell me, where does the audience sit?

I'd like to have a word with the director
I'm not too sure about the cast
I have some questions about the lines –
which come first, and what comes last?

I'd like a sideshow between the acts
There's choreography I'd like to practice
I'm improvising most of the time,
but what do I do if I forget my lines?

Where does the audience sit?
Where does the audience sit?
If all the world is a stage,
Tell me, where does the audience sit?

relax

relax
relax
    let your worries float away
relax
relax
    you can leave them behind, 'cause they

        just clog up your mind
        with feelings unkind
        you can lighten your load
        if you leave them behind

forget
forget
    your stress and fear aren't needed here
forget
regret
    cherish this time and hold it dear

        Life washes over you
        love fills your soul
        you've always known something new
        making you whole

relax
relax
    let your worries float away
relax
relax
    and let yourself enjoy today

Girl Trouble

You knew I wanted you, the first time I saw
you in your hippie shirt without a bra
My head it spun and my eyes crossed
When you walked in, I was at a loss

My soul was on fire
with a feelin' of desire
now I want you so bad
when you don't make me mad

    Girl trouble in my heart
Some days I feel I never see your face
Sometimes I start to think I need more space
Just when all the little pieces are fallin' in place
    The whole thing falls apart

Sometimes I know, sometimes I don't
Sometimes you will, sometimes you won't
Sometimes I think we're out of touch
Sometimes I think I think too much

The vortex starts to shrink
Can we find the missing link?
I don't want you to feel used,
But I think we're both confused!

    Girl trouble in my heart
Some days I feel I never see your face
Sometimes I start to think I need more space
Just when all the little pieces are fallin' in place
    The whole thing falls apart

Wanderin' (Where the Clouds Touch the Snow)

Oh, I've been wanderin' in search of gold
but it never, never, never ever saved my soul
And I've been wanderin' high and low
I wandered where the clouds touch the snow

And I've been wanderin' all through this town
I walked this city's streets lookin' up and down
For I've been searching, I'm trying to find a way
Yeah, I'm still longin' for some bliss every day

I took a lot of wrong turns

I crossed the ocean, and the desert sands
but I still haven't found out who I am
And I've been wanderin' all through this land
And I've been such a lonely, lonely, lonely man

Oh, baby, oh, don't you know,
Oh baby, baby, babe I miss you so
Oh, baby, oh, don't you know,
Oh baby, baby, babe, I love you so

Oh, babe.

Friends

One day I was thinking about my friends
Sometimes I get pissed off at them
but as I think more about it I see
sometimes they prob'ly get pissed off at me

There's a lot of things that make you who you are
Thanks for driving me around in your car
When I think of all the good times that we've had
I hope you know that I am really glad

Oh yeah, I'm glad!
I'm really glad
I'm glad to know you
I'm glad that you're my friend

We share a common bond of circumstance
maybe we share the future, or the past
sometimes we share a way of looking at things
sometimes we play games, or go out on evenings

There's a lot of things that make you who you are
and if you keep on tryin', I know that you will go far
When I think of all the good times that we've had
I hope you know that I am really glad

Oh yeah, I'm glad!
I'm really glad
I'm glad to know you
I'm glad that you're my friend

Part 4: A Year in Egypt

(2000-2001) – *Twenty-Five to Twenty-Six*

೮Ⴚ⋆ಹ

Cairo Sunset

The Cairo sun sets in a haze
Old men with brooms sweep the street
Echoes bounce from hill and edifice
The mournful sound of the call to prayer

The Dragon's Aftermath

Mental overload
feel you're going to explode
Gotta run, gotta run
I just wanna have some fun
Feel the wrath on the path
of the dragon's aftermath
Got a choice, so rejoice
now stand up and use your voice

The dragon is calling your name
Your life will never be the same

Watch it burn, watch it burn
maybe you will never learn
See the fire, feel the heat
'til you're dancing in the street
You fall asleep at night
and dream of the dragon's flight
with the dawn he is gone
but the damage lingers on

The dragon is calling your name
Your life will never be the same
You feed the fire of the dragon's wrath
And watch your life burn in his aftermath

Voices

Don't believe everything you hear
Someone's sellin' the same lies year after year
Ignorance breeds faith, and faith breeds fear
Don't believe all that they tell you, think about what you hear

If you wanna change your life, throw your old life away
If you wanna be yourself, be yourself every day
If you wanna be a fool, then be a fool and be proud
If you wanna play some music, you can play it really loud

'cause you are crazy from the voices screamin' in your head

Don't believe everything you hear
someone's fuckin' with your head, year after year
Swallow all their lies, and don't shed a tear
never ever show your feelings, or you'll always live in fear

They're watching what you do, and they hear everything you say
They send subliminal instructions to you each and every day
Don't ask too many questions, no don't step out of line
'Cause then you might get noticed, and they don't like your kind!

They'll say you're crazy from the voices screamin' in your head

Soulfire

Crawling away from the fire
that's burning in your soul
Always filled with desire
for something to make you whole

Looking deep into your eyes
I thought I could see the sun
So far beyond truth and lies
Too far no matter how you run

Still lookin' for a way to stop the screaming inside
You're crying for love, your heart is open wide

Nobody else will ever know
what you see when your eyes are closed
you gather energy from the moon and sun
and exercise the power of imagination

Twisting shapes that grow and fall
The reality in your mind
Thoughts that swirl and spiral down
The truth is not so hard to find

And maybe it doesn't have to make sense
but still, you are always asking, "Why?"
You can live your life in the present tense
Looking down upon the sky (from high up above)

And then you find a sunny day, your joy is bubbling inside
You laugh with love, your heart is open wide

Memory Loss

You know, I still remember you
all the things you used to say and do
I remember when it felt so right
and I remember how we used to fight

I will always carry in my mind
the good times that we left behind
Even though I have no regrets
I think now I should forget

That part of my life is now a part of the past
although sometimes I still want to see you again
It doesn't help to think about what couldn't last
so I try not to remember back when

I was with you, baby, all of the time
your eyes looked so deep into mine
Even though I have no regrets
I think now I should forget

I need to forget how I enjoyed our time:
the passion, the anger, and the bliss divine
I have to move on 'cause I don't want to pine
I am not yours, and you are not mine

The Voices in the Forest

There are voices in the forest,
    in the shadow, in the shade,
And they've whispered to each other
    ever since the world was made.

The wind cries in the treetops
    as they rustle up above
And it sings its sad lament
    searching for its absent love.

The birds, as through the air they wheel,
    cry out their lonely cry,
"We could suffer an eternity
    but still we'd have to die."

Still the singing of the insects
    fills the silence in my ears;
Yet *their* cry is but a lust for blood,
    and their death brings me no tears.

But down there in the shadows
    where the mold and mushrooms grow
I sometimes hear a whispering,
    perhaps from far below.

It speaks to me of time long gone
    and days still yet to come;
It sings to me of summers long
    and magic spells undone.

I've gazed into the shadows,
    but no speaker there I find.
I fear the voices whisp'ring
    are but voices in my mind.

I gaze to the lonely treetops
    and my longing eyes implore
But they speak to me no secret,
    they'll be silent evermore;

Save when the wind is blowing
    or a bug may chance to sing,
Or the winding wood may hear the call
    of songbirds on the wing.

My lonely heart calls them all dear
    but my soul, it longs for rest.
Tho all these whispers call me near
    I still love yours the best.

Overflow

Just when I thought my life was all in its place
    you came along and tore it apart
Just when I thought my mind was done with its race
    you came along and stole my heart

Maybe you didn't mean to
but now I can't stop thinkin' of you

I shout at the sky
    when I feel I'm gonna overflow
You know I try
    to breathe and let it all go
I keep asking why
    you've set this hook in my soul
But baby I
    don't even know if you know

Yeah you got me babe, if you want me I'm here
    Yes I'm a man with you on my mind
So come to me girl, and let my kisses make clear
    It's time to leave your worries behind

All my sorrows won't mean much
'Cause you can heal me with your magical touch

I shout at the sky
    when I feel I'm gonna overflow
You know I try
    to breathe and let it all go
I keep asking why
    you've set this hook in my soul
But baby I
    don't even know if you know

Listen

Now I know what went wrong
My expectations misled me all along
Wisdom is found in adapting my plans
Because the future is not in my hands

When I can dream, baby, it's all right
But thoughts of you keep me up at night

Oh, I listen to the words you say
Oh, I think about them every day
Oh, maybe I can convince you to stay
Oh, if I can make things go my way

You don't know the power that you hold
You determine how the story will unfold
You can make me smile or cry
I hope you never say "goodbye"

When I can dream, baby, it's all right
But thoughts of you keep me up at night

Oh, I listen to the words you say
Oh, I think about them every day
Oh, maybe I can convince you to stay
Oh, if I can make things go my way

Feel the Groove (a Happy Funk)

People, it's time for you to get up and dance
as if this were the end of the world.
Everybody everywhere has a smile on their face
they know that what they're seeing is absurd.

You've got to be free, got to relax your mind
and let that criticism fly away.
You've got to be free, got to be who you are
and live your life for today.

Live, live for today
Don't give, give your life away
Just live, live for today

Don't feel shy and small, just stand up straight and tall!
Your eyes are open, saying you are proud.
You already know how, so move your body now
just like you've got your head in the clouds.

Time is going by, you can forget if you try;
don't think too much, just let your body move.
Tomorrow's not here yet, yesterday is just the past,
so let yourself feel the groove!

Feel, don't you feel the groove
So let, let your body move
Feel, just feel the groove

Behebik

Ana behebik, wu owz ashoofik
   tamaly.
Alitool keda, enti helwa
   auwi.
Ya habibti!

Enti mish sekna fi Amrika,
   la'a, la'a, la'a.
Qalby bitaaik, Ana eizik,
   aiwa, aiwa.
Ya habibti!

Heya ismaha, "hiyati"
Heya ismaha, "Ya habibti, yalla!"
Heya ismaha – eh da?
Heya ismaha, "Ya habibti, yalla!"

Ana ediki al wegud.
   Owza eh, habibti?
Maarafsh musta'bil.
   Behebik keda, walahi!
Ya habibti!

Enti aarfa Ana maaish
   felouse kitira.
Bikellum "Yalla," mafiche moushkella,
   mish aandi aarabaya kibira.
Ya habibti!

Heya ismaha, "ishta"
Heya ismaha, "Ya habibti, yalla!"
Heya ismaha – eh da?
Heya ismaha, "Ya habibti, yalla!"

Enti bes, enti bes,
mafiche had teni gherik.
Enti bes, enti bes,
mafiche aya wahad teni.

Khalas.

Part 5: Barnlife

(2001-2003) – *Twenty-Six to Twenty-Eight*

ೞ✿ೲ

Natural Selection

Oh, I'm a child of the galaxy
I can see what's in front of me
I don't believe what they say on TV
Their indiscreet subjectivity

Life ain't always the way that you want it to be
    natural selection and genetic diversity
but it will balance out, ideally
    that's how it is, and how it shall be
The birds of the air eat the fish of the sea
    they told me about it at the university
The cycle moves on continuously
    Natural selection and genetic diversity

Well, all my life I've wanted to be free
to choose my joy and my misery
I don't need approval from society
to put my feet on the path I see

And everybody's ready to criticize
    But you're free to be the way you always wanted to be
They'll fill your head with their guilty lies
    They told me about it at the university
They thought I would never realize
    Natural selection and genetic diversity
That I can see with my own two eyes
    peace and love are inside of me

Old Magic

There's an old magic that's rising
up from the fields
And the eyes in the bushes
know just how you feel

You can feel it, you can smell it
You can taste in every breath
There's a sense of urgency
Like uncertain life or death

There's a rustle and a whisper
And a swooping rush of feather
As you stumble through the jungle
In a dream that lasts forever

There's an Old Magic
        in these trees
There's an Old Magic
        surrounding me
There's an Old Magic
        deep in the woods
It's got Soul magic
        like a forest should.

Never

I've lost my concentration,
can't think about anything.
In my imagination,
keep hearing the phone ring.

She told me that she loved me,
and then she went away.
I'm trying to hide all of my feelings inside
'cause it hurts to think about her all day.

And I'm tired of sitting on the floor
and staring at the wall
trying to convince myself
that she's never gonna call –

She's never gonna call!

She said she would always remember,
but I know she never gives me a thought.
She don't call, never, never
one chance with her was all I got.

Yeah, she's out there somewhere,
she's having a good time.
She's hanging out with people
who don't know that she once was "mine"

And I'm just sitting all alone
and staring at the wall
trying to get it through my head
that she's never gonna call –

She's never gonna call!

Feeling Down

There's a terror in your head
and it's filling you with dread
as you spend your whole life wishing
you were someone else instead

There's a fear in your heart
as the world falls apart
You're trying to start over
but you don't know where to start

There's a feeling in your town
that the shit is going down
and when it all goes up in flames
nobody wants to be around

Hopelessness fills the air
guns and hatred everywhere
you feel the panic rise
behind your cold and blankened stare

You're feeling so down
Down, down, down, down

This is where it all begins
there's no atonement for your sins
You're gonna feel this guilt forever
'cause nobody ever wins

You hear the ticking of the clock
can't get through your mental block
as if all your love and joy
have been frozen into rock

Lost in depression and in shame
cannot speak a good friend's name
You've lost all your connections
You will never feel the same

because nobody understands
there is nothing in your hands
While this emptiness consumes you
and spreads out across the land

You can't turn your life around
Down, down, down, down

Back Up!

You know, it really hurt when I fell down
My face was smashed right into the ground
I tripped and fell, it felt so bad
My thoughts of you had made me so sad

So I pulled myself together
and I reached for my cane
and now I'm back up, I'm back up,
back up on my feet again

Oh, ay, oh, ay,
I'm back up on my feet again
I refuse to stay down my friend, no way
No way, no way,
When circumstances make me fall
I'll jump right back and stand up tall again
That's what I say
I'll try so hard with all my might
So everything will come out right, my friend
There is a way
To scale the cliff and win the fight
And find a love to hold tight in the end

I thought that I had lost my way
I despaired of returning to the light of day
My life seemed to have all gone by
And all I could do was hang my head and cry

So I slapped myself hard
and I called out your name
For I will never give up hope
that I will see you again

Oh, ay, oh, ay,
I'm back up on my feet again
I refuse to stay down my friend, no way
No way, no way,
When circumstances make me fall
I'll jump right back and stand up tall again
That's what I say
I'll try so hard with all my might
So everything will come out right, my friend
There is a way
To scale the cliff and win the fight
And find a love to hold tight in the end

The Ballad of the Country Fair Girl

Once I met a girl
    who was too good to be true.
It's a beautiful story,
    I'll tell it to you.

It was a sunny afternoon
    one Sunday long ago
I was at the Country Fair
    I was dancin' at a show

It began at 4:20
    when the Orchestra Dark Star
Sent me tripping through my mind
    I must have gone pretty far

Because I didn't really see her
    'til she was right next to me
With her long dark hair
    and her cut-off blue jeans

Well, she looked so pretty
    in the afternoon sunlight
And the day it was just perfect
    the band sounded just right

So we danced, she and I,
    exuberantly
We built up and shared each other's
    energy

We were dancing together
    although we never had met
I thought I should say "hello"
    but no, not just yet...

For I was not there looking:
    I'd had one too many mess!
I'd no plans to try to hook up;
    although I must confess

that many years ago, I sang
    a song that I once wrote
in a key I don't remember,
    not even just one note:

It said, "I'm waiting for the girl
    with flowers in her hair
She said she'd meet me by the bridge
    at the Oregon Country Fair!"

Yes my heart was oh so ready
    though my mind it was still cold
But when the show was done
    before a second had grown old

The beautiful girl, she slipped away
    disappeared into thin air
and I thought I'd never find her
    at the Oregon Country Fair

Oh, you can dream so many dreams
    but never chase them down.
I thought that I would never see
    my Dream Girl around.

But neither sun nor stars
    had marked the passage of much time
Before I saw her again
    while I was waiting in a line.

She stopped and stared at me
    while I waited for the bus,
And I stared back at her
    not much distance between us

But she was walking with some guy,
    so I thought I should not try
To approach her just like that,
    for he'd prob'ly knock me flat.

So I let them pass me by
    but a moment later I
Turned around to see
    her walk away from me!

She had approached me from behind
    while I stood there in that line,
But she never made a sound:
    it was too late when I turned 'round!

I should have caught up with her then,
    but I could not think of what to say
So I just watched my Dream Girl
    as she walked away

I cursed myself
    as I rode on the bus
How could I have missed
    an opportunity thus?

For when she had walked up to me
    I had not seen her there,
And so I never met the girl
    from the Oregon Country Fair.

I pondered and I wondered
    as I rode on home
How could I get my Dream Girl
    to call me on the phone?

So I put an ad in the newspapers
    in Portland and Eugene,
And said I'd like to see her
    if she would like to see me.

My friends were all quite skeptical.
    The man at the paper: "You know,
There were lots of sisters with butterfly tats
    dancing at that show."

But she saw my ad, and she called me!
    She wasn't sure if it was real;
She said, "You described a girl in a blue shirt,
    but the one I was wearing was teal!"

    ·

We'd been the same places
    and thought the same things
We felt the same magic
    and dreamed the same dreams

Sometimes things work out
    if you take a chance –
Yes, sometimes you get to meet
    the Dream Girl from the dance.

Do Me No Wrong

Baby, I miss you,
    you know I wanna kiss you
        it feels like you are so far away
My world's fallin' apart,
    but I know in my heart
        that I want to be with you every day

You make me feel so good
    just like a man should
        when you say those sexy words to me, baby
But now I feel so alone
    and I want you to come home
        my thoughts of you are driving me crazy

Now I toss and turn
    and lay awake all fuckin' night
Tryin' to make myself believe
    that everything's gonna be all right
Baby I just hate it
    when you go away for so long
But I know you, my love
    and you won't do me no wrong

No, you won't do me no wrong
I know, I know
you won't do me no wrong
No, no, no, no, no, no, no

You're the moon in my sky
    I love the way you shine
        you light up my world in the night
When I look in your eyes
    I always recognize
        that everything is gonna be all right

Though I miss you, my love
    there are stars up above
        I wish upon them, and I think of you
I will be with you soon
    my night will turn to noon
        and our love will feel like it's brand-new

Baby I just wanna hear
    your voice on the telephone
Tellin' me you love me,
    and that you're comin' home
Babe I bet you wonder
    what I do when you're away
But my mind is with you, woman,
    I think about you night and day

And I won't do you no wrong
My love, my love,
I won't do you no wrong
No, no, no, no, no, no, no

Answer Machine

Hey, Jenny, I leave a message on your answer machine,
Hey, Jenny, I wanna talk about the places you've been.
You can tell me the story of your day,
Why this is a great place to be, and why you'd like to go away.

Hey, Jenny, I'm not like the other guys
And you're a beautiful young woman with a sparkle in your eyes
Well, I've met a lot of people, from Walla Walla to Kathmandu,
But it's been a real long time since I've met somebody like you.

Well I know that I ain't perfect, but I'm pretty goddamn good!
I'm trying really hard to live my life the way I should.
Hey, Jenny, I'm hoping you will see
that we'd have a good time, because you are a lot like me.

Hey, Jenny, we could have a lot of fun,
You and me, playing games in the sun
Hey, Jenny, whenever you are free
I'd love to hear from you, so I hope that you will call me.

Part 6: Portlandia

(2004 to 2009) – *Twenty-Nine to Thirty-Four*

ॐ

The Key to Happiness

Well, somewhere on the other side
there's a door that happiness hides behind,
and you can knock and scream and plea
but it won't open without a key.

There's a thousand trials to endure before
you get to stand before that secret door:
a test of endurance, of speed and skill,
a test of fortitude, a test of will

For you have got to suffer before
You can unlock that secret door

With the Key to Happiness
the Key to Happiness
the Key to Happiness
Lookin' for the Key to Happiness!

Somewhere on the other side
Oh, yeah, you can take a ride
as soon as you find, but not before
the key that opens that golden door

Well, some say it's hookups, and some say it's gold,
but sooner or later they both get old –
you got to find it within, you can't take it from me,
yes everybody's got to find their own golden key

and you must find your key before
you can unlock that secret door

with the Key to Happiness
The Key to Happiness
the Key to Happiness
Lookin' for the Key to Happiness!

Vishnu's Dream

Matter is made of energy that flows through the Universe
Everything is energy that flows through the Universe
All that there is and all that we see is the flowing of energy
Everything is energy that flows through you and me

 For I am part of you
 and you are part of me
 and we are part of everything
 and everything is part of Vishnu's Dream

Everyone is part of everything, connected in unity
The energy of the Universe is flowing through you and me
We are all part of everything, and everything is part of us
Light is made of energy in this infinite Universe

 For I am part of you
 and you are part of me
 and we are part of everything
 and everything is part of Vishnu's Dream

Matter is made of energy that flows through the Universe
Everything is made of energy that flows through the Universe
We are all part of everything, and everything is part of us
Life is made of energy in this infinite Universe

For I am part of you
and you are part of me
and we are part of everything
and everything is part of Vishnu's Dream

Lazy Sunday Afternoon

There ain't no better way
just to pass the day
    doin' what I'm doin'
    and smilin' while I'm groovin'
it don't matter what the people say

Adjust my attitude
now I'm in the mood
    Feelin' those rhythms
    and move along with 'em
I'm gettin' down in the groove

I'm just lazin' away on a Sunday afternoon
Doing my thing, going nowhere in my room
    I don't know why,
    but time goes by
and pulls me with it all too soon

You know I love the rain
They tell me I'm insane
    Let it water all the grass
    while I sit here on my ass
bloomin' flowers in my brain

You know I love the light
but I stay awake all night
    Let the daylight and the sun
    shine down on everyone
and make everything all right

I'm just lazin' away on a Sunday afternoon
Happy to have put off all of my things to do
    I don't know why,
    I'm going to try
to climb my way up to the Moon

Global Neighborhood

There's too much sadness in the news
  Nobody knows what we can do.
It's all 'bout pain, oppression and fear,
  I really wish everyone could hear

That we all just need to love each other
  and treat each other like we should
We all just need to love each other
  and spend our lifetimes doing good.

Well we could all live together in peace
  respecting the land, the air, and the seas
Creating a world in harmony
  with lots of forests full of trees

We all just need to love each other
  and treat our Earth Mother like we should –
We all just need to love each other
  brothers and sisters, global neighborhood!

Soapbox

Standin' up on my soapbox preachin'
never know if my words are reachin'
You, or you, or anyone, anywhere;
can you tell if the world is still unaware?

Things are never quite what they should be
it's a lesson down through history
Together we can change society
if we start right now with you and me

Try to save the green environment
try to save my right to be a dissident
Try to save the right to choose
we've lost a lot, but there's still a lot left to lose

War mongering administration
intelligence manipulation
Intentional misrepresentation
in the United Nations

They wanted a war
and more, and more, and more
a never ending war

because they profit from the war,
they profit
blood and bombs just boost their bank accounts
they profit from the war
they profit
blood, and gold, and oil by the ounce

Ask questions in the Home of the Brave
while we still have some freedom left to save
You don't have to be a commie
to believe in a rational economy

Education, universal healthcare,
put an end to this class warfare.
Every job should pay a living wage,
even though the corporations rage!

Worst time since the Great Depression
the result of Republican oppression
the politics of rich and poor
they're always wanting more and more

Hey, those laws against the terrorists?
Speak your mind, and you'll get on the list!
The government will tap your phone
They'll read your email when you're not at home

Keep my speech free
give me privacy
just let me be
how I want to be

because it's my fucking life
it's my life
so take your fucking wiretap off my phone
it's my fucking life,
it's my life
go away and leave me alone

Just let me be
In privacy
I want to be free
Without society
Telling me
What I can and cannot do
What's it to you?

I'll keep going, always another thing
for the love of freedom let me sing
I want everyone to understand
so a better world they will demand

Tryin' to be careful what I eat
Fruits, veggies, and free range organic meat
We shape the world with what we buy
so make good choices, or we'll all die

Just live sustainably, please
Stop choppin', save some trees
World warms, the glaciers melt
Worst thing humans ever felt

Work together for a real solution
I'm tired of breathin' pollution
Express your resolution
Strengthen the Constitution!

The rule of the many
The rights of the few
here's what we do
it's up to me and you
because

we've got to change the world
we've got to
things just can't keep going like they are
we've got to change the world
we've got to
for future generations and for ours

Finding the Path

O goodness for which we strive
    for the betterment of self and all
Fill our hearts with sacred light
    and drive out darkness therein
May we find peace
    and turn away from anger
May we be forgiving
    in the face of wickedness
And through our understanding may we bring
    a better world into being

Asking Forgiveness

May my transgressions be forgiven
  though I know I have done wrong
I vow to learn from my mistakes
  to make such atonement as may be made
And to lead my life henceforth purposefully
  putting past evils behind me
Setting my eyes upon the
  attainment of balance

Sunset

The sunset over the mighty river
Is sinking down below the trees
The warm scent of the flowers and whatever
Carried on the evening breeze

Ooh ah
The gentle evening breeze

The rocks and stones of this great mountain
Are piled high into the sky
Listen to the echoes of the insects calling
To each other in the fading light

Ooh ah
The evening's fading light

As the light of the day
fades into the dark of the night
See all the stars so far away
all shining so bright

A Guide
(An Incomplete Versification of an Early Version of My Philosophical Treatise)

I. Foreword: Moving Forward

The wise man will not accept my words
    just because I say them;
the wise woman will want to think about my ideas
    to see if they fit in with her own.

Praise be to the wise!

For though I may feel strongly
    about the beliefs I have expressed herein,
        my understanding of the Cosmic All is limited
    to my own sphere of existence.
Certainly scientific advances
    and human experiences in the future
will reveal much that is hidden from me.

I am a bard and a scribe,
       though I have dabbled
           in many professions.
I have studied diverse subjects,
    both in school
    and in life;
and I have traveled
    within the country of my birth
      as well as abroad
        to Europe,
          the Middle East
           and southern Asia.

In my childhood
    I was educated by Catholics;
in my mid-twenties
    I lived among Arabs for a year.
I count among my friends
    many Pagans
        and Buddhists,
            as well as Christians, Muslims and Jews.

I am a citizen of the United States of America,
    the most powerful country in the world.
As I write this,
    America is at war
        overseas,
    struggling to recover
        from economic recession,
            and suffering
                from internal strife.
I am disturbed
    by all this pain
        and animosity,
    and by what I perceive
        to be its underlying cause:
            a power grab
                by the elite class of wealthy citizens,
                    who own the majority of the land
                    and the majority of the corporations.

I have thought long and hard
    about these and many other issues facing humanity today;
and I believe that many of them
    are the same issues that people will be facing
        for centuries to come.
In the interest of overcoming these issues,
    I would like to propose
        a philosophical framework
            which, I would like to think,
                most reasonable people would largely agree upon.

Based as it is
    upon both
        my studies and
        my personal experiences,
    the viewpoint I describe
        is not so much a new way of seeing,
        as it is a unification
            of several worldviews
        to make a colorful,
            dynamic,
                yet simplified understanding
                    of an infinitely complex reality.

In additional to such philosophical ponderings,
    herein you will also find
        my practical suggestions
            for several ways
                in which we might make our world
                    and our societies
            more livable in the future.
The crucial point
    behind these ideas
is my firmly held belief
    that people can unite the power of their wills
        to consciously create
            positive social change.
    Consciously changing the world
        to make the future better than the present
    is the greatest human ambition,
        and great things
            will be achieved
                when all the people in the world
                    learn to see
                        who they are,
                        when they are,
                        and what they can do.
When we learn to work together
    in a spirit of cooperation
    in pursuit of joy,
        then surely the fruits of our labors
                will be a world which we have improved.

Take these thoughts home
        and think about them,
                my brothers and sisters;
        and laugh at them,
                if it please ye;
        but think about them
                all the same,
and then pass them on
        to your friends,
                and to your children.

                        Your brother in Peace,
                        Jesse Smith

                II. Creation: A brief, anthrocentrist synopsis

In the beginning,
        there was nothing.
But the absence of being
        implies being;
                and thus,
                        from the remotest edge of probability,
the infinite universe sprang into existence.

Many people give a name
        to the Force which creates Being,
                which is itself Being;
and because there are many people,
        there are many names for God.

Given an infinite number of worlds
        and an infinite period of time,
                having filled the void
                        with the dust
                                of exploded stars,
the Great All manifested itself
        in boundless possibilities and combinations.
On our planet,
        one unusual combination
                became possible
                        in the mineral-rich "primordial soup"
                                of the shallow seas.

As the waters were bombarded
    with cosmic radiation,
a random chain
    of amino acids
        formed into a double helix,
          and learned how
            to replicate itself.
This was
    the origin
      of life
          as we know it.

Sing praises!

Creation is vast and bountiful.

Sing praises!

The infinite cosmos
    is unpredictable
      in its beauty
        and its manifestations.

Hallelujah!

Various life forms are
    colorful,
      wonderful,
         beautiful,
    multi-faceted,
      strange,
        bizarre,
    and sometimes
      dangerous
        or ugly,
           even revolting.

O the wonders!

The experience of life itself
   is wonderful,
   beautiful,
   confusing,
   bizarre
   and sometimes
   extremely unpleasant.

O the splendors!

After life forms
   had evolved
      and diverged
         and gone extinct
            for hundreds
               of millions
                  of years,
a certain small family of primates
   from the continent now known as Africa
found that it had been endowed
   with a unique set of genetic traits.
These relatively hairless proto-humans
   began to walk upright,
      made tools and weapons,
        and eventually
            evolved an unusual capacity
               for self-awareness
                  and communication.
This, then, was the origin of Mankind,
      and be it known that we are as the animals,
        and they are like unto us,
     for we all follow
         the chaotic mathematical guidelines
            of the Cosmic Oneness,
               which we live in,
                  and of which we are made.

Sing praises!

A Request to the Muses

O Fortune, thanks! I have been blessed.
    I humbly do request
the Muses me to grant
    the words that I shall chant.

For not a one may quarrel
    with this obligation moral
to expostulate at length
    until the end of all my strength

Upon a subject so splendid
    it never will be ended,
and superseded? Never!
    A love that lasts forever.

When U Dance

You know I love the way you move
    when you dance
You shimmy and you shiver
    and you jiggle and you prance
You know I love the way you
    shake that thing
It makes me want to laugh and cry
    and jump around and sing

Baby you're so groovy when
    you get down
You're the funky little smokin'
    dancin' cutest thing around
Baby when you're movin'
    all the men fall down
You're the groovy hottie crazy
    sexiest thing in town

Nothing I Would Rather Do

Once upon a time there was a girl,
    the most beautiful lady in the world.
The sunshine sparkled in her eyes,
    the crickets sang her lullabies .

Once upon a time there was a boy,
    all he owned in the world was his voice.
He sang a carefree song
    wherever he went, all day long –

He sang, "Ooh, la la, shoo be doo, wah wah
  Ooh, do be do, there's nothing I would rather do."

One day the boy was walking through the town
    his head held high as he skipped across the ground
His song surrounded him wherever he did go,
    he sang of following the rainbow.

The young lady chanced to hear him as he passed,
    His song captivated the young lass
And though she had never heard the song
    She joined right in and sang along:

She sang, "Ooh, la la, shoo be doo, wah wah
  Ooh, do be do, there's nothing I would rather do."

Now the boy and the girl sing together,
    Pledging to each other every day 'til forever.
Their days and their nights are filled with love,
    Their song lifts up to the stars above.

They sing their song in perfect harmony,
    They sing their song knowing they are free,
They sing their song all across the land,
    They sing their song walking hand in hand

And they sing, "Ooh, la la, shoo be doo, wah wah
  Ooh, do be do, there's nothing I would rather do!"

Wedding Blessing

We call upon the earth, the sky, the water,
and the living energy of the universe
to witness and bless this union.

We are children of the Earth,
for we are made of the elements of the Earth,
and the Earth sustains us as we walk upon it.
We trace our romantic relationship back
to shared celebrations of nature and its cycles.
We offer our blessings to the Earth,
and call upon the Earth to bless this union.

We are children of the sky,
for we live in the air and breathe it
as a fish in the sea breathes water.
The air sustains us, and blows us through
the unpredictably beautiful chaotic weather of our lives.
We offer our blessings to the sky,
and call upon the air to bless this union.

We are children of the water,
for the water of life flows through our veins
and quenches our thirst.
Rain and streams make the world verdant with life.
We are proud to celebrate our union here,
near the great ocean.
We offer our blessings to the water,
and call upon the water to bless this union.

We are children of fire,
the Spirit, the great unknowable cosmic energy
that creates time and space. The very matter
which weaves the fabric of the universe
is made of energy:
energy which also expresses itself
as the Sun, which nourishes life with its rays
and warms our home;
energy which also expresses itself
as complex chemical reactions
such as fire, and consciousness.
The Sun warms us, and makes crops grow.
Fire warms us, and makes technology possible.
These are but a few expressions
of the infinite nature of the Force.
We offer our blessings to fire, to the Sun, to God,
and call upon these to bless this union.

Faded Blue

Every day
workin' for my pay
Every night
she makes me feel all right

Everything she does
the best there ever was
She don't even care
we own nothin' but air

I gotta make things right
cause I'm getting a fright
How can I pay the rent
when the money's all spent?

Beneath the stars
wearing the stripes
I've been workin' for the man all my life
Blood red with white
and faded blue
honey tell me what we're gonna do

Every day
Standin' on my feet
Every night
I try to make ends meet

Every day
workin' at my job
Every night
I tell her not to sob

I gotta make things right
cause I'm getting a fright
how can I pay the rent
when the money's all spent?

Beneath the stars
wearing the stripes
I've been workin' for the man all my life
Blood red with white
and faded blue
honey tell me what we're gonna do

Hear the neighbors fight through the apartment wall
try to drown it out with the TV
Can't afford to leave, can't stand to stay
Thank God I am free!

Beneath the stars
wearing the stripes
I've been workin' for the man all my life
Blood red with white
and faded blue
honey tell me what we're gonna do

Might Not Be Tomorrow

Sometimes I don't know
what we're gonna do
no place to go
options are few

So many ills
I'm tryin' to forget
with all these bills
and so much heavy debt

It's hard to say,
"everything will be okay"
But we will find another way
Life will be better someday

It might not be tomorrow
or even the next day
but put aside your sorrow
and wipe those tears away

I don't get enough
take home pay
I want to go on
holiday

I can't replace my busted things
with stuff that's new
but baby we will
make it through

It's hard to say
"everything will be okay"
but we will find another way
life will be better someday

It might not be tomorrow
or even the next day
but put aside your sorrow
and wipe those tears away

Hope

The littlest things
seem to have no meanings
from the weirdest of dreams
to the song the bird sings
the truth of it all
from the Spring to the Fall

Leave your sorrow behind
there's still more to say, because
love gives hope to the disarray

Explanations swell
and fill a deep well
with the love and the light
on a cold Winter night
to fill up the soul
with a soft warm glow

Leave your sorrow behind
move t'wards a new day, because
love gives hope to the disarray

Elves

Well, it's no mean little thing
when a man begins to sing
he's gonna put his heart out there on the line
and tell you everything

The dusty tales of history
their sadness and their mystery
and the paths of all the stars
and terraforming Mars

All his dreams and all his goals
and all the scars upon his soul
his love and his obsessions
all his dreams and his possessions

The random images that come to mind
are spinnin' round on spiral lines
swirling and resolving
and flowing throughout time

Flying over trees and houses
drifting through the clouds
that are floating through the air
above the old time country fair

And in the distance glimmering
Your goddess beckons shimmering
she tells you she can show
all the things that you don't know

And it's no secret to the fishes
who are living in the lake
no, it's no secret to them, not at all
for they make no mistake

And it's no secret to the creatures
of the forests and the mountains
behind the bushes, thorns, and stones,
and statuary fountains

It's no secret to the birds
who are flying through the air
but the people just go walking by
completely unaware

Of all the elves who peek out
from behind every leaf and bloom
frolicking and capering
from midnight until noon

And the gnomes who tunnel underneath
the roots of every bush and tree
will ride upon the squirrels
as they lead the way to victory

Through dewy fields beneath the stars
that twinkle beyond counting
swirling fractal mathematics
of nature's magic mounting
to the sky above
with a giant love

Watch the shining snowflakes
that are falling just like kisses
on the trees and ground and all around
the whispering of wishes

That are sometimes granted right away
They come to see the light of day
like dewy raindrops falling down
and flowing through the waterway

While through the rosy waterfall
of dawn we count our blessings
as a thousand forest nymphs
let down their hair and start undressing

In a wooded glen, remember when
we were livin' out our dreams
We built a rosy kingdom
with cooperating teams

We captured all the monsters
and we put them in a bag beneath the stairs
so they will never catch us
sleeping unawares

And now the days are sweet
and filled with pillow-fluffy memories
that hide behind electrons
and fill all the world with our
giant love
to the sky above

Part 7: Getting Down to Business

(2009 to 2015) – *Thirty-Four to Forty*

Everything is Perfect

Everything is perfect
Everything is perfect, baby
    and you are so beautiful to me

I couldn't ask for a better
I couldn't ask for a better, baby
    I could not ask for a better, no, no, no

'Cause life is beautiful
Life is beautiful
Life is beautiful with you here

And everything is perfect
Everything is perfect, baby
    Everything, everything

The Graphic Design Song

Here's your canvas, here's your fill
    Now's the time, exert your will
You know that you're up to the task
    when you apply a layer mask
It's like when you assume a disguise
    but you don't have to tell no lies
    just the story hidden in your eyes

Set your blending options
    and add transparency
It's the way you fit in with society
    blend in with transparency
Yeah I'm standing right over here
    but you still can't see me
    no you just look right through me

Duplicate your layer style
Choose something to make you smile
Always doing your very best
So you go that extra mile

Add some texture and some relief
    There's some shadow, coz there's always more grief
Add some highlights and a bit of glow
    your light shines from within, you know

Gonna Make It

Gonna make it
gonna make it
yeah, we gonna we gonna we gonna we gonna make it

And we'll find it
yes, we will find it
yeah, we gonna we gonna we gonna we gonna find it

'coz we are ready
to carry on
like the song

yes, we will sing it
yeah, we gonna we gonna we gonna we gonna sing it

and we are naked
yes, we are naked
yeah, we are all we are all we are all gonna get naked

'coz we are willing
all along
to show that we're strong

yes we are gonna
yeah we gonna we gonna we gonna show that we're strong

and we will make it
yes, we will make it
yeah, we gonna we gonna we gonna we gonna make it

'coz we are ready
to carry on
already gone

Part 8: New Directions

(2016 to 2019) – *Forty-One to Forty-Four*

ങ⚕ഇ

Changed Me to Other Directions

In new directions I travel
Of travels in new directions I sing
Not merely inspired
Relentlessly pursued
By those divine Muses
who compel my pen
to write these words
of its own volition:
the pen moves my passive hand.

Their inspiration
whirls me on
to new things,
casts me headlong
into another
massive project
that will probably
take me years
to complete.

Introduction to 'Arthur is Dead'

Hear my most tragic tale of love, loss, and life,
    Of glories and failures and plans,
And I will tell you of the gentlest of knights,
    Uniter of all the sere lands.

Sir Arthur the bold, who was brave and strong,
    Aspired to such lofty goals,
He forged on ahead, and he brought us along
    To chase fleeting ephemerals.

Gone are the bright summer days of our youth
    When he and I played in the fields,
Gone are the days when we fought for the truth
    Like brave, bold knights bearing our shields.

He rode up so high into the blue sky
    Upon Dame Fortuna's grim wheel
'Til thru treason and lies, he failed and he died;
    And my guilt, I shall not conceal.

For Arthur is dead, and on my own head
    The world heaps the guilt and the blame.
Sometimes I wish it had been me instead
    As I live on in my grief and shame.

Now Arthur is dead, he is passed far beyond
    To rejoin the Earth Mother again.
Yes, Arthur is dead, and all hope is gone
    For a world in which people can be friends.

He is dead, and the hope of our era dies too,
    We know that he cannot return;
With no resurrection, it's now up to you
    To learn from this what you may learn.

He is dead, and likewise our hopes and dreams fare
    That buoyed us through these dark times;
He is dead, and our lives are plunged into despair
    It's burning a hole in my mind...

He is dead, and the memory plagues me by day,
    My brother's warm smile and firm shake;
He is dead, and the madness is not far away
    As I lie in my bed, wide awake.

Almost as though I had killed him myself
    As though I had ended his life,
Almost as though I had killed him myself,
    My brother, his future so bright.

Almost as though I had killed him myself
    By stabbing his heart with a knife;
Almost as though I had killed him myself
    The day I first slept with his wife.

So a warning to you, dear friend as you set
    Your eyes on this page the first time:
My sorrowful tale full of woe and regrets
    Shall list these laments line by line.

And it gets really nasty, e'en lewd in places,
    Full of things you'd not say to a stranger:
Tho it be noised about by the radio faces,
    It's not meant for your younger teenager!

Passion Storm

Every time you call my name
Every time you walk away
Every time we dawn a new day
It's a passion storm

There's a time for callin' your name
There's a time for walkin' away
There's a time to dawn a new day
It's a passion storm

Everything that you wish for, baby
Everything that drives you crazy
A hurricane of your kisses, lady
Blowin' up a passion storm

Every time you shake it, baby
Don't you know that you drive me crazy
'Coz you're one hell of a woman, lady
It's a passion storm

Gotta tell you sweet woman I love you
And I'm never gonna let you go
'Coz it's written in the stars above you
It's a passion storm

Desolation Danger

Desolation danger
Don't be a stranger

Hope for the best
    you don't have to feel down
Maybe there's time
    to turn it around

Desolation danger
Don't be a stranger

Babe if you gotta go
    I hope you'll come back around
We'll bury your problems
    six feet under the ground

Desolation
It's misery without you here
In danger of fallin' down
That's why I need you to be near

Desolation danger
Don't be a stranger

Feelin' the fool
    feelin' the clown
Maybe it's time
    to get out of town

Upside Down

The world is upside down
it's upside down,
it's up, it's down,
the world is over
it's upside down

Stole the teeth from Cadmus
so long since I had this
overflow with gladness
everything, everywhere

The world is upside down
it's upside down,
it's up, it's down,
the world is over
it's upside down

Descent into madness
always filled with sadness
weighted down by the badness
that fills the air

The world is upside down
it's upside down,
it's up, it's down,
the world is over
it's upside down

All my plans
just fail and fail
I try so hard
but lose the trail
Nothing works
it falls apart
all the wrong words
and an aching heart
Where did it go
where does it lead
What do you know?
Nothing, indeed!

Meteorite

Wishing on a falling star --
interstellar dust that's traveled so far,
until it bursts into flaming light:
a burning arc across the starry night.
You know, I sympathize...

And then you flame out
yeah you flame out
Like a meteorite, a meteorite
You're out of range
you're out of bounds
Yeah you're out of sight

Comet particles and dust
burn up in the upper atmosphere
when interstellar paths collide
at this time of year.
And I wish you were here...

And then you flame out
yeah you flame out
like a meteorite, a meteorite
You're out of range
you're out of bounds
Yeah you're out of sight

We're spinning 'round a star
And all the other stars
are really really
really really far away...

And then you flame out
yeah you flame out
Like a meteorite, a meteorite
You're out of range
you're out of bounds
Yeah you're out of sight

Learn to Love

You say you don't want to hear about politics
Oh no you just can't stand the thought of it
The very mention of the word just makes you sick
You say you're so tired of divisiveness

Well, maybe there is a simple solution
that will not require a violent revolution

We gotta learn to love
    love, love, love, love
don't push and shove
    we gotta learn to love
try to rise above
    gotta learn to love
The one thing there's never enough of
    is love, sweet love

Too many people discriminate
They go around with hearts filled with hate
Come on people now, it's not too late
Let's come together and celebrate

Come together and celebrate
Maybe it is not too late

We gotta learn to love
    love, love, love, love
don't push and shove
    we gotta learn to love
try to rise above
    gotta learn to love
The one thing there's never enough of
    is love, sweet love

The Farm

Up on the hill behind the house
there was a giant oak tree
where my dad built a tree fort
for my sister and me.

Nearby was a moss-covered shed
where my mom raised sheep:
lambed them, wormed them,
and sheared them for their fleece

Down on the farm
where I grew up

There was a giant wooden barn,
it was a century old,
with a hay loft, and horse stalls,
and a pen for the pigs we sold.

We raised chickens, and a goat,
we rode horses through the woods.
We ate vegetables from the garden,
we weren't rich, but life was good.

Down on the farm
where I grew up.

Beautiful Heart

Beautiful heart
Nothing will keep us apart
Walkin' in the sunshine
Glad to know that you're mine

Beautiful heart

Don't know what I'd do without your love, baby
My glue, my compass, my star
Standin' on my feet lookin' at the sky above, baby
Thinkin' 'bout how wonderful you are

Beautiful heart

There's a Magic Around You

    Patience
gets us through when things don't
    make sense
I'm on a roll but baby it's
    all downhill
    maybe I'd be better standing still

    Baby
do you know what you mean
    to me
you're the one I love, that's why
    I wrote you this song
    I hope you've known all along

That I'm so lucky I found you
There's a magic around you
Sparkles glitter in the air
ev'ry time that you are there
Flowers bloomin' in the place
where the light shines on your face

You've seen me happy
You've seen me sad
You've seen me good
You've seen me bad

And through it all
Though it's hard to see
Somehow you've
put up with me

Oh can't you see, oh can't you see

That I'm so lucky I found you found you
There's a magic around you round you
Sparkles glitter in the air
ev'ry time that you are there
Flowers blooming in the place
where the light shines on your face

Keep Dreamin'

Well, darling, I plan
to be a good man for you
        baby I want you to stay
I'll never forget
I'm so lucky I met you
        and baby I want you to stay

The birds all sing
in trees of green
We live in a dream
But it's the best thing I could dream of
so I guess I'll just keep dreamin' of you

So hitch a ride home
and endure my poems
        coz baby I want you today
We'll go for a walk, and
I'll listen to you talkin'
        coz baby I want you today

The birds all sing
in trees of green
We live in a dream
But it's the best dream I could dream of
so I guess I'll just keep dreamin' of you

Better and Better

You know, we're often tired at the end of the day
You know I don't always have too much to say
Honey I hope you know I'm so glad to have you here
Sitting right beside me, let me hold you so near

It's getting better and better
and better and better
with you, ooh
baby you, ooh

Baby everything you do is good
I try to treat you like I should
Fill our home up with love
La la la la la la, la la la love

It's getting better and better
and better and better
with you, ooh
honey, you, ooh, yeah

Our troubles are worlds away
Happiness is a game we play
I love you more each day
You know it will be okay

Keeping hope alive
Shine a light on the darkness inside
Baby you got me feelin' all right
Why don' cha come see me tonight

It's getting better and better
and better and better
with you, ooh
baby you, ooh

Things just keep getting better
the longer we're together
It's getting better with you
and everything you do

the end
*of one phase
is the beginning
of the next*

Appendix A: Copyright Notes

Copyright note: The following works have been previously published, released, and copyrighted:

The songs, "The Greeting," "Armor Amour," "Gonna Be OK," "Flowers in Her Hair," "What U Got," "Minimum Wage," "Sunshine Spy," "Rainbows of Sound," "Stupid Jerks," "Affirmation," "Aliens," and "Alone" were included on the self-produced recording project, *Basement Recordings Inc. presents Sweet Dreams*, copyright 1997.

The poem "A Koan" is from the complete version of my short story "At the Center," original copyright 1998. The story was published in the literary magazine *Blue Moon* in 1998 as "Excerpts from At the Center," but the published excerpt did not include this poem. The complete version of "At the Center" is also included in the short story collection *Perspectives*, copyright 2020.

The songs, "Carryin' It," "Sing It," "Duncan's Quest," "Penury," "The Lover's Madrigal," "Armor Amour," "Flowers in Her Hair," "Aliens," "U-B-O-K (formerly known as Gonna Be OK)," "Sunshine Spy" and "The Pensive Pooch" were included on the self-produced recording project, *Basement Recordings Inc. presents Mush – the Porphyritic Album*, copyright 1999.

The songs, "Armor Amour," "Sometimes Closer," and "Carryin' It" were featured on the 3-song demo album, *JUT*, also featuring Tom Kay on bass guitars and Ulysses Martinez on drums, produced and engineered by Brent Rogers, copyright 1999.

The songs, "Armor Amour," "Do It Now (Start the Day)," "Dream Confessions," "Duncan's Quest," "Faceless Man," "Girl Trouble," "Paradise Regained," "Sometimes Closer," "Spunky Haste," and "Wanderin' (Where the Clouds Touch the Snow)" were included on the

The poem printed here as "A Guide (An Incomplete Versification of an Early Version of My Philosophical Treatise)" includes text from Chapter 1 of my self-published manifesto, *Principles for a Self-Directed Society*, copyright 2008 (second edition 2020).

The songs "Behebik," "Faded Blue," "Might Not Be Tomorrow," and "Feeling Down," were included on the self-produced album, *Flumergex Emerges*, copyright 2011.

The songs, "Elves," "Everything is Perfect," and a number of the others (as remakes) appeared on the self-produced recording project originally titled "*Jesse Smith 'Live' at the Buffalo Ranch*," copyright 2013. (This project may someday be released under the tentative name, *Flumergex: Just for Fun.*)

The poem "Introduction to 'Arthur is Dead'" was composed as the introduction to my as-yet unpublished novel, *Arthur is Dead*, copyright filed in 2016.

The songs, "Hope," "Gonna Make It," "Passion Storm," "Desolation Danger," "Upside Down," "Meteorite," "Learn to Love," "Beautiful Heart," "There's a Magic Around You," "Keep Dreamin'" and "Better and Better" are slated to appear on the forthcoming album, tentatively titled, "*Flumergex: Too Much! Songs from Rock Bottom*," copyright 2019. (The song, "Learn to Love" has the same melody as the song, "Jon Objects" from *Flumergex Emerges*, copyright 2011.)

A brief clip of an uncredited instrumental performance of the song, "Minimum Wage" was included on the soundtrack of an indie movie whose name I have forgotten. The movie was produced and directed by a guy named Ira, who was a friend of our drummer, Ulysses Martinez. The recording also featured the brilliant Tom Kay on bass guitar. The movie was never picked up for broader distribution, but it showed at The Hollywood Theater on Sandy Boulevard in Portland Oregon in the early months of the year 2000. The indie movie itself, as well as its cast, crew, producers, and soundtrack, are all missing from IMDb; but it was a strange and wonderful experience nonetheless.

Appendix B

In closing, I would like to share with you the oldest poem I discovered while compiling this collection.

I wrote this last poem when I was in the second grade, in the school year 1982-83, when I was about 7 years old.

It was not a strong enough piece to open this entire collection; but as personal history, I could not bear to omit it completely. So I include it here for fun, and with this bring the collection full circle.

Thanks for joining me on this journey! I wish you well.

A Song

River run to the sea
If you need someone
    you can run to me

Flowers grow to the sun
You know it shines
    down on everyone

Lean back on a star
Feel as big and strong
    as you are

Lightning Source UK Ltd.
Milton Keynes UK
UKHW021933050922
408396UK00003B/95